In Memoriam

In Memoriam

Henri J.M. Nouwen

Ave Maria Press • Notre Dame, Indiana 46556

Acknowledgments:

Short scripture quotes from Jerusalem Bible.
Psalm 41 from the Grail translation.

© 1980 by Ave Maria Press, Notre Dame, Indiana 46556

Library of Congress Catalog Card Number: 79-56690
International Standard Book Number: 0-87793-196-8 (Cloth)
0-87793-197-6 (Paper)

Printed and bound in the United States of America.

$\mathcal{M}$y mother died on Monday, October 9, 1978, at 6:14 p.m. It was one of the few moments when I was not at her bedside. I had just left the hospital room to make a telephone call. When I reentered the room, my brother looked at me and said, "She is dead." My father had put his head on the bed and was crying softly. My sister and younger brother, who had been standing outside the room talking, came in and looked at her silent face. It was over now.

The doctor came in, listened to her heart and said, "Yes, she has died." Then we prayed. I struggled to find the words which were our words: words of grief, words of gratitude, words of hope. It was a very intimate moment. My mother lay there, still and in peace. Looking at her, we prayed, "Lord, lead her now to your house and give us the courage to continue our lives, grateful for all she has given to us." Then we left the room where we had spent the last five days, hour by hour witnessing her pain and struggle. We knew that she would never be with us again.

I want to write about these last days with my mother. So much happened in those days that I fear it will escape me in the whirlwind of everyday life unless I can find words to frame my experience. I want to express how during those days her love, her care, her faith and her courage became more visible to me than ever before, and how I came to know in a new way what it meant to be her son. But it is so difficult and painful. Every word seems to be the wrong word, every expression seems to do violence to what I feel, every page of praise or gratitude seems to distort that gently built network of love that was her life. Yet, not writing is worse; not writing is like not mourning, not feeling the pain, not tasting the bitterness of her farewell.

I know that it would be possible to continue, telling myself that she died as we all have to die; to be brave, strong, self-composed and firm. I know how to answer the condolences of friends who say, "I am sorry to hear that your mother died." I have my sentences ready: not so many as to bore them, not so few as to appear abrupt or cool. By now, I have used them many times: "Thank you. . . yes. . . it all happened faster than we thought . . . she and my father came to visit me in the United States. . . when she arrived at Kennedy Airport she felt very tired and could not eat. . . the doctor, a friend, found jaundice caused by a tumor. . . she returned with my father after only four days. . . in Holland she underwent surgery. . . the cancer proved widespread . . . she regained consciousness following the operation but died six days later from a complication in her lungs. . . ."

I have no idea how often I have uttered these insignificant phrases. Why do I repeat these empty sentences? They explain nothing. Worse, they seem to hide more than they reveal. Every time I use these words I keep wondering why I am so unable to communicate the mystery of which I have become a part, the new vision that has disclosed itself to me. The endless dialogue, "I am sorry". . . "Yes, I am sad," often touches off a strange weariness instead of bringing comfort. Even so, I am deeply grateful to everyone who expresses sorrow and am quite eager to share my grief with anyone. But something is taking place that is too important to be confined to the few phrases that I have already used so often. I must try at least to say more.

My mother died. This event cannot claim any uniqueness. It is among the most common of human experiences. There are few sons and daughters who have not experienced or will not experience the death of their mother, suddenly or slowly, far away or close by. Still, I want to reflect on this event because, although it is not unusual, exceptional or extraordinary, it remains in many ways unknown and unfathomed. It is indeed in the usual, normal and ordinary events that we touch the mystery of human life. When a child is born, a man and woman embrace, or a mother or father dies, the mystery of life reveals itself to us. It is precisely in the moments when we are most human, most in touch with what binds us together, that we discover the hidden depths of life. This is the reason why I feel free now to speak about my mother, whom I have loved so dearly and whose death is causing me such deep grief. In many different ways she has told me, and still tells me, that what is most universal is also most personal.

I remember how embarrassing it always was for my mother when I would praise her in the presence of others. She did not like me to speak about her. But now she no longer holds me back; she can no longer be embarrassed. Now she is no longer just my mother; she is a woman whose son wants to speak about what she has revealed to him, not only in her life but also in her death. In life she belonged to a few, in death she is for all.

1

*I*t all happened so fast—and slow! As I flew from New York to Amsterdam, I realized that I was going to say farewell to my mother. As often as I had made that same trip, this time it seemed unreal. Already I felt my perceptions changing as my immediate surroundings seemed to fade away. I had a hard time listening to the pleasant lady on my right who told me about her daughter's college. I could not bring myself to buy earphones to listen to music or to follow the sound of the movie. I could not make myself read a book that would draw me into the complexities of other people's lives. Above the cold North Atlantic, I felt alone. Not lonely, not depressed, not anxious, not afraid, but alone in a new way. My mother was dying. She was waiting for me to come, she wanted to see me and to pray with me. It was this reality that began to fill my mind as the plane carried me home. I realized that something very new was happening to me.

Just a month ago I had been flying from Jerusalem to Rome. A sixty-year-old man sitting next to me explained that he was returning to the United States to attend the funeral of his brother. I remember feeling uncomfortable, somewhat embarrassed and self-conscious. I even felt some irritation because I had to sit for three hours beside this man with whom I could not have a "normal" conversation. Now I was the one who might embarrass or irritate my fellow human beings, people who did not want to be pulled out of their joyful anticipation of a happy holiday. I realized that sorrow is an unwelcome companion and that anyone who willingly enters into the pain of a stranger is truly a remarkable person.

At seven o'clock in the morning I finally walked through the long hallways of Schiphol airport. Two hours later I entered the hospital room in Nijmegen where my mother lay in pain. From the moment I saw her I knew that something totally new was beginning. I smiled and she looked at me, grateful that I had come. I kissed her forehead and touched her hand. Words were hardly possible or necessary. The only thing that seemed important was that we were together.

She was looking at me with the same eyes with which she had so often looked at me—when I went to the seminary, when I became a priest, when I left to live in the States: eyes expressing a love that could never be separated from pain. Maybe that was what had always touched me most deeply—her eyes, in which love and sadness were never completely separated. How often had I seen tears in her eyes when I left again after a day, a week or month at home! How often had I looked into that lovely face, which expressed so beautifully that love causes pain!

I can still see her waving from the quay of Rotterdam Harbor as the large ship *Statendam* slowly left its berth, taking me on my first trip to the United States. I can still see her waving as I passed the "passengers only" sign and walked through the airport gates. I can still see her waving from the door of the house as I was driven away in my brother's car. And—the clearest memory of all because it happened hundreds of times—I see her waving from the platform as the train rolled away from the station, making her figure smaller and smaller and smaller.

Always there was a smile and a tear, joy and sadness. From the moment of my birth when her tears merged with smiles, it has always been that way.

Now there was no doubt that she was dying; it was so clearly written on her face. I knew that we both knew. But there were no words. I bent over her face. So close, so intimate, so gentle, so painful. The tears in her eyes made me realize that while she was glad that I had come, she was also sad that we could now do no more than just look at each other—and pray.

"Shall I pray?" I asked softly. She seemed pleased and nodded. Knowing she would have asked me this if she had had the strength to speak, I realized that the words of the psalms would make it possible to communicate with each other in new ways. For a year now we have prayed with the same prayerbook. During the many evenings we spent together we had read the hymns and psalms of the evening prayer, finding in them a time of shared tranquillity. When I opened the book it was all so very normal, familiar and safe.

Like the deer that yearns
for running streams,
so my soul is yearning
for you, my God.

My soul is thirsting for God,
the God of my life;
when can I enter and see
the face of God?

My tears have become my bread,
by night, by day,
as I hear it said all the day long:
"Where is your God?"

These things will I remember
as I pour out my soul:
how I would lead the rejoicing crowd
into the house of God.

Why are you cast down, my soul,
why groan within me?
Hope in God; I will praise him still,
my saviour and my God. (Psalm 41)

As these words were slowly shaped by my lips,
covering her like a gentle cloud, I knew that we were
closer than ever. Although she was too ill to smile,
too weak to say thanks, too tired to respond, her
eyes expressed the joy we felt in simply being
together. The psalms had a power which I had not

recognized before. They lifted the veil of sentimentality. As soon as the words of the psalms were spoken, there was a strength, a power, and a divine realism between us. There was a joyful clarity. A mother was dying, her son was praying, God was present and all was good.

As she looked into my eyes, I knew that my gratitude for her presence in my life would live on within me. As I looked into her eyes, I knew that she would die grateful for her husband, her children and grandchildren, and the joyful life that had always surrounded her. "Why are you cast down, my soul, why groan within me? Hope in God; I will praise him still, my saviour and my God." There was a surge of energy that did not come from an ailing woman or a heartbroken man. There was a sense of truth that embraced us both. I did not cry or feel the desire to do so. She did not cry or try to say a word. We were together in a moment of truth, a moment that we wanted to taste together.

How long would it last? How many hours, days or months would we be able to have together? "Why worry about it?" I thought. "Why not simply be here to taste and see the goodness of the Lord at this very moment?"

Then I kissed her again and said, "I am going to get a few hours' sleep. I need it after the long plane trip. I will see you tonight." I pressed a sign of the cross on her forehead with my thumb and added, "Good-bye . . . sleep well." Then, after quietly leaving her room, I went to the house where my father and sister were waiting for me. I felt very peaceful, very strong, very joyful. We were together, and we were surrounded by strength.

2

When I returned in the evening her eyes had changed. I looked at her but she could no longer respond with her eyes. I pressed her hand but she could no longer hold mine. My brother and sister were with me at her bedside. I said, "Mother, I want to give you the sacrament of the sick. . . . I want to give you the oil of healing and we want to pray for you together." I bent over her and she said softly, "It is hard for me to think, you know what is good." After lighting a candle, I prayed for healing, for new life, for strength in this moment of crisis and for the courage to surrender to God's will. It was at this moment, when I crossed her three times with the oil as she lay quietly on the bed, that I realized she had turned her eyes to God.

Until this hour she had been thinking and speaking about us, her husband, her children, her friends. Now it seemed that the time had come to face God. Her eyes had turned inward. She no longer saw her husband Laurent, and her children, Harrie, Paul and Marja, Wim and Heiltjen, Laurine and Marc. She was seeing other realities, more awesome, more frightening, more captivating, but also more decisive.

Shortly after this quiet moment—the intimate celebration with a burning candle, a few softly spoken words and the touch with oil—the struggle began. We were not prepared for it; we had never even thought about her death as a death with a struggle. We had not anticipated anxiety, fear and agony. Why should we? Hers was a beautiful, gentle, generous life, marked by giving all there was to give. It could not possibly end in a restless, painful, torturous struggle. Peaceful people should die a peaceful death; faithful people should die a quiet death; loving people should die a gentle death. But is this true? Who am I to formulate simplistic equations and logical sequences? Since I do not even know why we live, why should I expect to know how we are to die? If life is a mystery, why should death

be viewed as a reality within our grasp and understanding?

The soft oil I had given her was much more than
oil that points to healing. The apostle James certainly had healing uppermost in his mind when he wrote:
"If one of you is ill, he should send for the elders of
the church, and they must anoint him with oil in the
name of the Lord and pray over him. The prayer of
faith will save the sick man and the Lord will raise
him up again; and if he has committed any sins, he
will be forgiven" (James 5:14-15). But oil is not only
a symbol of healing. It is also a symbol of struggle.
Ancient warriors anointed their bodies before battle,
and modern-day wrestlers use oil to limber their
muscles and make their bodies agile.

Could it be that I had applied oil on my own
mother to help prepare her for the final battle? Is it
not possible that she who lived her life in such close
union with God had also come to know the power of
the Evil One more intimately than many others? Is it
inconceivable that she who had spent so many hours
in prayer was also most aware of the one whom we
call "the Tempter"? Is it not possible that great
faith reveals the possibility of doubt, that great love

reveals the possibility of hate and that great hope reveals the possibility of despair?

I began to realize that the oil I had given her was a sign that a great battle needed to be fought. Indeed, it is the ultimate battle, the magnitude of which is understood by only a very few.

This is more than a pious attempt to explain a difficult death. Mother had told me not just once, but often, that she was afraid to die. Many people will say the same, but mother meant something very concrete, very specific, very unambiguous. Three weeks before her death she said to me, "I am afraid to die, not to go to the hospital, not to undergo surgery, not to suffer pain. I am afraid to appear before God and show him my life." It was this great encounter that frightened her. She was so deeply impressed by God's awesome greatness and had become so aware of her own nothingness that the great encounter could only frighten her.

Maybe *fear* was not the best word; perhaps she meant *dread,* the overpowering knowledge of the great abyss between God and his creatures. That awesome awareness meant a momentous struggle, a battle, a fight. How can a human being face God and live? What is there to hold on to except faith, hope and love? Everything else seems to vanish in this terrifying hour—even husband, children, grandchildren, and a beautifully lived life with its joys and pains. At the moment of death only God matters. The struggle is a lonely one. Indeed, the oil is a profound symbol at the hour of death.

Shortly after I had given the sacrament of the sick to my mother, she entered into a long, drawn-out agony. My brother, who had decided to stay with her a little longer while my sister and I went home, saw that the quiet peacefulness had left her and that a restlessness had started to take over. Not only did mother's eyes no longer seem to focus on those around her, but her movements no longer had a specific direction and her whole body appeared to be gripped by fear. When my brother told me what was happening, we decided that from then on we wanted to be with her every moment of the day and night. We followed her agony from minute to minute, from hour to hour, from day to day.

How great is the mystery of our life! Not one of us had suspected that we would be witnessing this painful struggle of the woman we loved so much. There was nothing we could do except be there, hold her arms, which moved restlessly in the air, gently wipe her perspiring forehead, and carefully fluff up the pillows, offering every little bit of comfort we could.

I still wonder what I was feeling during those hours. I felt powerless, small and helpless, but also peaceful, strong and quiet. I was seeing and feeling something I had never seen or felt before, an experience that to be described would require words that have not yet been found: powerless yet strong, sad yet peaceful, broken yet whole. I still do not fully understand this new emotion. One thing, however, I can articulate because I felt it so clearly: I was blessed to be part of a moment of truth.

Everything was truthful, there was no lie. Mother was dying and nobody denied it. Although her suffering was deep and mysterious, it was not hidden from us. We experienced the privilege of being close to her suffering, intimately connected with her pain, deeply united with her agony. Looking at mother's blank eyes, guiding her restless arms in their haphazard movements, and repeating words of consolation and comfort, I was not afraid, I was not anxious, not nervous, not self-conscious. I have never felt so strongly that the truth can make us free. It was a very sacred moment, and I was blessed to be there.

The world outside—the cars on the streets, the voices in the hospital corridors, the students in the United States, the lectures to give, the conferences to attend, the articles to write and the books to discuss—suddenly appeared illusory and permeated by shadows of untruth. The truth was here, now, in this room: mother was dying, in mortal struggle with the great powers of life and death.

She no longer saw me or my father, my brothers, or my sister, but she saw what we could not see. From the depths of her struggle she cried out to God, "O God, my God, my Father, my God." These words—words she had said thousands of times during her life—now came from the center of her being and formed a long, agonizing cry.

As the long hours passed into longer nights and days, her cry became deeper and stronger. Bending over her, I heard her words of prayer: "My Father who art in heaven, I believe, I hope, I love. . . . My God, my Father. . . ." I knew that this was the struggle of the great encounter. I wanted to give her the freedom she needed to enter into this lonely hour, to give her the space where this most mysterious of events could take place. I knew that she needed more than comforting words; she needed whatever support we could give her in this struggle of faith. With my father, brothers and sister, I prayed the prayers she hinted at—the Our Father, the Creed, the Hail Mary and the Litany of the Mother of God. In this way, we felt as if we offered her the words she could no longer speak herself, surrounding her with a shield of prayer that allowed her to fight her lonely battle.

Why? Why were we witnessing such pain and agony in a woman whose life had been one of goodness, gentleness, tenderness and love? Why did she who had been so generous and self-giving have to enter into this torturous hour? Why all this pain, this suffering, this struggle?

During the days of mother's dying, I heard that question repeated frequently. Often, friends suggested that it was unfair for this lovely woman to suffer such a painful death. Many were adamant that she did not deserve such a wrenching struggle. But do we really understand?

Slowly, as the long hours and days passed, I began to wonder if mother's struggle did not in fact reveal the awesome truth of God's love. Who was more loving than Jesus? Who suffered more than he? Jesus' life of faithful service did not end in a peaceful, tranquil death. He who was without sin suffered an agony of immeasurable depth; his cry on the cross, "God, O God, why have you forsaken me?" still echoes down through the centuries.

Is it this agony that mother was called to share? Is it this cross that she was invited to feel more deeply than many others? I do not know. I cannot say yes or no to these questions. What really took place during the hours of her death cannot be explained or made understandable. But the thought that she who had loved so many, given so much and felt so deeply, was called to be united with Christ even in his agony, did not leave me during these days.

Friends kept saying to me, "Your mother always thought of others first." That is true. She lived for others: for her husband, her children, her grandchildren, her friends. She indeed had the mind of Christ, always considering the other person to be better than herself. But that does not necessarily lead to a smooth death. Why do we think that Christian death is an easy death? Why do we believe that the hope for a life with Christ will make our death like a gentle passage? A compassionate life is a life in which the suffering of others is deeply felt, and such a life may also make one's death an act of dying with others. When I saw mother's battle, her cry of hope and faith, I wondered if she was not crying with the many others for whom she had lived.

In Jesus' agony we see the agony of the world in all its gripping intensity: "Sadness came over him, and great distress. Then he said. . . 'My soul is sorrowful to the point of death' " (Matthew 26:37). Is not every human being who wants to live with the mind of Christ also called to die with the mind of Christ? This can mean very different things for different people. It certainly does not have to mean the struggle mother suffered. Yet it seems at least important to understand that those who live with Christ must also be prepared to die with him, to be willing even to accept the invitation to enter into his agony.

What then is this agony? Is it fear of God, fear of punishment, fear of the immensity of the divine presence? I do not know, but if I have any sense of what I saw, it was more profound. It was the fear of the great abyss which separates God from us, a distance which can only be bridged by faith. The test comes when everything that is dear to us slips away—our home and those we love, our body and its many ways of living, our mind and its caring thoughts—and there is absolutely nothing left to hold on to. It is then that one must have the faith to surrender to a loving Lord, to believe that he will not allow us to fall into a cruel and bottomless canyon, but will bring us to the safe home which he has prepared for us. My mother knew her weaknesses and shortcomings. Her long life of deep prayer had not only revealed to her God's greatness, but also her own smallness; not only God's openheartedness, but also her own fearfulness; not only God's grace, but also her own sinfulness. It seemed that it was precisely her lifelong conversation with God that made her death such an agonizing event. At the hour of death all becomes faith. Faith in God, who knows every fiber of our being and loves us in spite of our sins, is the narrow gate which connects this world with the next.

What am I talking about? Am I making an existential drama out of the death of a woman who lived a good life but died a painful death? The doctors and nurses in the hospital, who surrounded my mother with competent care, neither could nor would speak with the words and concepts that I have been using. They referred to a growing lack of oxygen, a hard-to-explain restlessness and a difficult-to-understand groaning. But is that all there is to say? No doubt lack of oxygen creates anxiety, but not all anxiety is experienced as a struggle of faith in the moment of the encounter with God himself. What am I saying when I speak about a sharing in Christ's agony? Some, mostly the medical staff, interpreted her struggle primarily as a physical response to a very radical operation. Others, who had known her piety, perceived it as the emergence of old memories and deeply embedded routine phrases repeated during a state of semi-consciousness. But I saw something else. I saw my own mother entering into that moment in which we are totally alone with God, in which the final decision of life must be made: the decision of faith.

3

How will things be and feel when she is no longer part of my life? Over the years I have often asked myself this question, even though I realized that there was no answer because the experience was so totally unknown. I became aware that during the years of my childhood, adolescence and adulthood, the bonds with my mother had grown so deep and so intimate that I would never be able to know their full significance before her death. Every time I tried to think of my life without her, my mind went blank, leaving me completely unable to imagine anything. But increasingly I sensed the mysterious depth of the relationship between mother and child. I had read enough psychology books to know about possessive mothers, dependent sons and deep, unresolved ties between children and parents. Yet I realized that all this failed to explain our relationship; there was much more to be understood.

From her I had come to feel an unqualified acceptance which had little to do with my being good or bad, successful or unsuccessful, close by or far away. In her I had come to sense a love that was free from demands and manipulations, a love that gave me a sense of belonging that could be found nowhere else. It is hard to express exactly what I was sensing, but the word "belonging" comes closest to it. She represented a reality of goodnesss and safety which was much larger than herself. When, even in the midst of turmoil and restlessness, conflicts and failures, I continued to feel that life is ultimately good and benign, I knew that she had been, and still was, my teacher. It had very little to do with frequent visits, letters or telephone calls; it had even less to do with discussing issues or making plans; and it had nothing at all to do with day-to-day decisions. With the Atlantic Ocean separating our homes, there were few occasions for the simpler forms of dependency.

When I thought to myself, "It is better to live than not to live, it is better to struggle and fail than not to struggle at all," I knew that she had something to do with it. Maybe I can say that she gave me that basic sense of the goodness of life that allowed me to move freely and fearlessly to many places, to live with many different people and in many different circumstances, and to feel free far from home.

If I had told her any of these things, she probably would have felt confused, embarrassed or even offended. Or perhaps she would have simply called me a sentimentalist. The fact of the matter is that I could not have said any of this to her. It is only now, after she has gone, after she has been buried, that these thoughts and words do not seem silly or romantic to me. They are simply the expression of a truth.

I never did arrive at an answer to the question, "How will life be when she is no longer present on the horizon of my thoughts, feelings and emotions?" Now I realize that I have to grow into the answer slowly, gently, carefully and very patiently. The answer will not come in the form of a thought or an insight, but in the form of a new love.

As I looked at my father, my brothers, and my sister standing around her in the hospital, I began to realize that she would never abandon us. That deep sense of safety she had given to us, that feeling of belonging to a world which could be trusted, would not die with her but would anchor itself more deeply in our being.

I saw this first in my father. I had often worried about his sorrow and grief should mother die before him. I had often wondered about his life alone after a long and happy life with her. But when I saw him looking at his dying wife, I realized that there were hidden resources that I had not seen before. It was the strength of a love which cannot be destroyed by death. I saw power, courage and freedom breaking through his tears. It was then that I knew that mother's death would not crush him. I also saw this same strength in my two brothers and their wives, in my sister and her husband, all of whom radiated a care, love and concern that revealed far more than the sorrow of losing their dearly loved mother. I felt it in myself. I felt strong, yes, even strangely joyful, during these days. It was the joy of feeling a great love binding us together, a love which she had given us and which was not going to be taken away from us.

It is difficult to put into words what I want to say. Such words as "love" and "care" can so easily be interpreted in an emotional way, and yet none of us standing around mother's bed were ever very good at expressing our feelings toward one another. In fact, during these long hours of waiting, none of us said anything very new. The words were the same as always. Yet, as we watched her life slowly fade away, we all sensed that the bond between us which she had created was growing stronger and deeper.

This new closeness that we began to feel was something far greater than what is expressed by the remark, "You still have each other." We became for each other new people with new lives and new perspectives. Life started to reveal itself in new ways. I was not simply saying farewell to her; I was also letting go of something in myself that had to die. I also perceived this in my father, my brothers, and my sister. Old boundaries that had maintained certain distances between us were being lifted so that new intimacies could grow.

Only in this context is it possible for me to understand fully why it became so easy for us to pray together. As children we had prayed together before going to bed. Although we still pray together at table, it is only infrequently that we enter together into the intimacy of prayer.

But as we found ourselves gathered around mother's bed, our prayer was easy, free, spontaneous and natural. It offered us words of greater power and meaning than any of the words we could have said to one another. It gave us a sense of unity which could not be created by speculations on the nature of mother's illness or her chances of recovery. It provided a sense of togetherness that was more given than made, and it created a place in which we could rest together.

Some of the prayers we said were ones that mother had taught us as children, prayers that now came to mind again after years of absence. Some were prayers which had never been spoken before, while others were prayers which have been repeated over the centuries by men and women in pain and agony.

The prayers we said together became the place where we could be together without fear or apprehension. They became like a safe house in which we could dwell, communicating things to each other without having to grope for inadequate, self-made expressions. The psalms, the Our Father, the Hail

Mary, the Creed, the Litany of the Saints and many other prayers formed the walls of this new house, a safe structure in which we felt free to move closer to each other and to mother, who needed our prayers in her lonely struggle.

Thus the days and nights passed—a sequence of prayer, silence, and short conversations. We had a deep sense that she experienced our presence and could perceive the gentle rhythm of our prayers. Often we would move close to her and tell her that we were there, tell her about our love and our gratitude. But mostly we just remained silent. During the first days we had read books or magazines to pass the time. Now we simply looked at her, and at each other, letting the long hours of the days and nights deepen our presence. From this time on all that mattered was simply to be with her without asking or demanding anything.

*A*fter three days of struggle mother was exhausted. She no longer had the energy to fling her arms about in anxious movements; she could no longer even mumble prayers or cry out to God in audible words. The doctor who had seen her long, painful struggle said, "For her it has been like running up and down a long staircase for three days. Now there is no strength left."

We sat by her bedside, watching her breathing becoming shorter and shorter every hour. For three days we had been struggling with her, holding on to her from both sides of the bed, speaking words of comfort, praying quietly or out loud. In the past week there had been moments when we thought about the possibility of survival, brief fantasies that mother might somehow come back home and once again be with us. But, above all, there was the desire to see her open her eyes, smile, and say a few words.

The hope for a single moment of recognition, or perhaps just a few words, held us all in its grip. We kept asking ourselves and each other: "Can she hear? Does she know that we are all with her? Does she feel our love and concern? Can she understand anything we are saying? Does she sense that we are praying for her?"

Sometimes there seemed to be a small sign of recognition, a glimmer of understanding. But mostly her eyes remained without expression and her hands no longer responded to our touch. Father looked at her and then said softly, "I know there are so many things you would like to say, but you cannot—it's all right, we are with you." While he was speaking these words, I felt our immense desire for a response, just a little response, a word, a nod, a smile, a movement of the hand. It seemed that we were begging for more contact.

How great is the human desire for contact! After thirty, forty or fifty years of living together, with its innumerable conversations, discussions, and hours of intimate exchanges, we still wanted another sign. We were still hoping that maybe mother would bless us one more time. At times I felt guilty for desiring yet another gift from her who had given us so much. I even felt selfish and greedy. But the desire was there, strong and powerful, and we had slowly to accept that she had given us enough, more than enough.

As the hours passed it became clear that she was dying, that we would never again receive another word or gesture from her. Although we had known for the past three days that she was dying, now the awareness of finality began to touch us. There would be no new chances for expressions of thanks or regret, joy or sadness. There would be no opportunities to change anything. Never. Her life was coming to an end and our relationship with her was moving into the realm of memory. We realized that the way in which we had been her husband, son or daughter was now defined forever. The question was no longer, "How are we going to interact with her?" but, "How are we going to remember her?"

As we looked at her—totally exhausted from the struggle, breathing short breaths—we found our memories beginning to summarize all that had been. My father looked at me and said very quietly, "I see my whole life with your mother passing in front of

43

my eyes: the first time we met, our first happy days, our first little disagreements and conflicts, our hard days of working together, your birth and all that followed until now. . . . It just stands in front of my eyes like a small picture I can look at.'' Looking at him, I sensed the brevity of life in my bones: a flash, a moment, a breath. . . arrival and departure. . . yesterday and today. . . all compressed in one blink of an eye. There was immense tenderness in that moment, an intimacy that I had not known before. It was not a case of the wise speaking to the unwise, the old to the young, the experienced to the inexperienced. There were no longer wise and unwise, old and young, experts and untrained. Here in the presence of death, we were indeed the same, feeling our equality as a grace.

The end came very quietly. I had left the room to make a phone call while my youngest brother and my sister were walking in the hospital corridor, talking a little between the times they spent at mother's bedside. My father and younger brother sat on either side of mother's bed, following her breathing. It had become very quiet. The nurses had just rearranged the bed, washed mother's hands and face, and combed her hair. All had become very quiet.

It was six o'clock in the evening. Father looked at her with full attention, expecting that she might still live for many hours. But then he noticed a definite slowing down of her breathing, saw her neck muscle make two more movements, and realized that she had stopped breathing. Everything was still, very still. Father bent his head, kissed her hand and cried. Then he said to my brother, "She has died; call your brothers and sister." As we stood around her bed we prayed the same prayers we had said so often during the past days. But now I added for the first time the words we would say in the long days to come: "May eternal light enlighten her that she may rest in peace."

She had simply stopped breathing. That was all. With carefully chosen words, father told us about the final seconds of her life, how the end had come with a slight quiver of her neck. "It was hardly noticeable," he said, with a soft smile in his eyes. It had been so undramatic, so quiet. It had hardly been an event. For a moment I felt sad because I had not been in the room. But then I realized that I should be grateful that father and mother had been so close in those last moments. I recognized that it was a gift that he, and not I, could tell the story.

5

$\mathcal{I}$t was a foggy Saturday morning. When I opened the curtains of my bedroom and saw a thick mist hanging over the fields, I thought that for many people it might be hard to reach this small, isolated village. At eleven o'clock, mother's funeral would take place. Following the service we would bury her in the small cemetery on the site of the old church which had been destroyed in the war.

As I looked out into the mist, I tried to become fully aware of my feelings on this day. But it was difficult to come close to my own inner life. There was the sadness of the farewell, but also the gladness of welcoming the friends who were coming from many directions to join us in our prayer. This was the day to remind myself, my family and my friends that she had indeed left us, that she would no longer make breakfast, call our names, or appear with her gentle smile in the living room. I had to let the truth that she had left us descend deeply into my heart.

My mind returned to one of the most difficult and saddest moments of the week. It occurred when I returned with my father to our home. We had spoken quietly about her during the 45-minute drive from the hospital to the small country town where my parents have lived for the last eight years. When we turned into the road leading to our house, I suddenly felt a deep, inner sadness. Tears came to my eyes and I did not dare to look at my father. We both understood. She would not be home. She would not open the door and embrace us. She would not ask how the day had been. She would not invite us to the table and pour tea in our cups. I felt an anxious tension when my father drove into the garage and we walked up to the door. Upon entering the house it was suddenly clear to us: it had become an empty house.

The large living room with the familiar paintings seemed to have turned into a waiting room, the bedrooms into guest rooms, the kitchen into a cold, silent place. I wandered from room to room, and felt a shiver throughout my entire body. Everything that for years had spoken of her presence now reminded me of her absence. Everything that had always told me that she was home now told me that I would never hear her warm voice again.

I walked into her little study and saw the many family photographs. Looking at the pictures of my brothers and sister and myself which I had seen so often, I realized that they had suddenly become different pictures telling a different story. I sat at her desk and looked at some notes she had written in the days before she went to the hospital. Suddenly, I realized that she who had written me every week would never write me again. In a drawer I found my name written on folders and envelopes and realized how often she had thought about me as she sat there. Only now did I fully recognize that I had become a different man, a man without a mother, a man alone in a new way.

I asked my father, "Would you like a cup of coffee?" "I will make it," he replied. As we sat down with the cups in our hands, we felt for a moment as if we were in someone else's house.

That evening I picked up her prayerbook and asked my father, "Would you like to say the prayers

I used to say with mother when I was home?'' ''Yes,'' he said, and we prayed the evening psalms which she prayed before going to bed.

During the following days things in and around the house kept reminding us of her. The time between her death and funeral became one of discovering the many ways in which she had left us. What for years had been so obvious, self-evident and normal had now become a subject of memory. Often the small things seemed the most painful, the little customs which had become part of our life together: the way she set the table, the times she called us together for coffee, the hour she went to church. In this way, she kept dying in us every hour, every day.

When Saturday finally came, I sensed that the funeral and burial would be the first opportunity to let my mother's death become the beginning of something new, an occasion to share the first visible signs of new hope and new life. I even felt a certain joyful anticipation as I looked out over the misty fields. We would now celebrate her life, give thanks for all she had meant to us and include the people of the village, family members and friends in both our grief and our hope.

When the time for the service arrived, the village church was filled. Not only was every seat taken, but people were standing in the side chapels and even in the choir loft. As I entered the church and put on the vestments to preside at the service, I experienced something for which I have not yet found words.

I was about to celebrate the Eucharist for my mother, who had evoked in me the desire to become a priest and with whom I had celebrated the Eucharist innumerable times.

I was about to bless and incense her body as a last farewell to her, she who had blessed me often during her life.

I was about to announce hope and new life to all whom she had brought together here by her death, many of whom had not heard the good news of the Gospel for many years.

I was overwhelmed by the simple realization that this service, which I had dreamt about with anxious anticipation, was not an hour of fear and anxiety, but an occasion of peace and consolation. I was going to bury my own mother, speak about her to her friends, sing hymns of praise and thanksgiving to God, and offer bread and wine as signs of his enduring love for us.

The service was indeed a real celebration, just the way my father had hoped it would be. The words of the liturgy, the festive music, the songs of the congregation and the divine gifts of the Eucharist made this a moment in which the goodness of the God of life was affirmed and our sad hearts were lifted up in gratitude.

But perhaps even more than the festive celebration in the church, the walk to the cemetery flooded us with an immense sense of God's presence. After our words and songs it was nature's turn to sing God's praise in this hour of farewell. By the time we left the church with the casket, the mist had lifted, the sun had broken through and the green pastures were full of light. As the procession slowly found its solemn way to the cemetery, mourners became like dancers. The young horses galloping in the fields, the birds playing in the air, the poplars slowly swaying in the wind, and the cheerful sounds of children running up and down the street—all reminded us of the God of life. Even those who were still overcome by sadness and sorrow found themselves pulled away from their introspection by these unmistakable signs of nature's vitality. I had the feeling that this procession to the cemetery might be the shortest walk longest remembered.

Behind the cross walked my two nephews, little Marc and Reinier, too young to mourn but not too young to carry the bucket and the sprinkler with a sense of doing something important for their grandmother. In front of me walked the pastor of the church and my mother's oldest brother in their priestly vestments. Behind me, my brothers Paul and Wim, my brother-in-law Marc, and four neighbors carried the casket. I felt the presence of my father, my sister Laurine, my sisters-in-law Marja and Heiltjen, and Frederique my little niece. They followed the casket so closely that they could touch the flowers which covered it. As I walked I let my mother's silver rosary, which my father had given me the day before, pass through my fingers. It was hard to concentrate on anything specific. The sounds of the wind and the playful children intertwined with the sounds of the prayers arising from the long procession. It was sad and joyful, strange and familiar, old and new, serious and playful, very hard and very easy. I simply let these contrasting sensations merge in my heart and mind without trying to sort them out.

At the cemetery little more needed to be done or said. A simple prayer, a word of thanks and a silent look at the place to which I will return many times in the years to come. My final impression was that of flowers—white flowers, yellow flowers, red flowers and purple flowers. After everyone else had left, my father and I stood for a few moments gazing at these flowers which covered the small plot of land in which she now lay. Then and there I had to learn again that mother was dead, gone, no longer with us. Tears pushed themselves into my eyes, making me feel very alone and very sad. I could only repeat the words that have sounded through the ages: "May eternal light enlighten her that she may rest in peace."

Three days later I returned to the United States. Only two weeks had passed since I had left Kennedy Airport, but it seemed like ages. During the eight-hour flight I was overcome by a profound desire to sleep. The anxieties, tensions and fears, as well as the emotions of joy, gratitude and love, had so exhausted me that I just wanted to forget everything and be carried home.

But was I going home? As I walked through the endless passageways of Kennedy Airport, waited in line for customs and called a limousine for the trip to New Haven, I felt more like a stranger than ever. The busy scene of thousands of people coming and going was the same as always, but this time I could not help asking myself, "What am I doing here?

Why do I come to this foreign country? What is it that makes me live and work so far from those who care most about me?"

It slowly dawned on me that she who had followed every decision I made, had discussed every trip I took, had read every article and book I wrote, and had considered my life as important as hers, was no longer. Little by little I became aware that mother, although far away, had always been part of my wanderings, and that indeed I had viewed the world through the eyes of her to whom I could tell my story. I began to feel that the airport, the limousine, the long trip to my apartment and all the other small inconveniences had become emptier, less meaningful, even somewhat absurd, because the ever-present dialogue with her had suddenly come to an end. Even so, I still found myself thinking: "I should write her about this," or "She will love to hear that story when I come home for Christmas," only to realize that she would never again read my letters or hear my stories. What is the value of my trips, my lectures, my successes and failures, my struggles and joys, when my stories remain hanging in the air?

Returning to the United States was returning to

my grief. Of course I have my father, and he loves me no less than my mother did. Yes, there are my brothers and sister and my many friends who surround me with their love and interest. But now, as I returned, it was her absence that pervaded my feelings, and I knew that the time had come for me to learn again how to make this world my home.

When I finally entered my room well after midnight, I looked at her portrait on the wall, and noticed the many things she had given me over the last decade. I had a difficult time believing that just a few weeks ago she and my father were sitting in these chairs, talking about all the little things by which we express our love for each other.

The weeks that followed are hard to describe. Fatigue, sorrow, sadness and confusion were certainly part of it, but also joy, gratitude, new insights and beautiful memories. I had to fight the temptation to "get back to normal" too soon. I kept thinking about Dr. Richard Cabot who, the day after his wife died, gave a lecture "as if nothing had happened."

Indeed, I felt a certain pressure to view this as the ideal for which to strive. But circumstances prevented my following Cabot's example. Instead, I was able to spend some "useless" time by myself. This was important, for without it I could easily have slipped into the illusion that indeed "nothing has happened and nothing has changed." In a society which is much more inclined to help you hide your pain than to grow through it, it is necessary to make a very conscious effort to mourn. The days when those in grief wore dark clothes and abstained from public life for many months are gone. But I felt that without a very explicit discipline, I might be tempted to return to "normal" and so forget my mother even against my will.

But I know that I must not forget, that I must remember her even if remembering brings with it pain, sorrow and sadness. The disciples of Jesus kept themselves isolated from the people for forty days, trying to comprehend what had happened. This long period of mourning was necessary before they were able to receive the Spirit. Only after this long and painful grief were they able to receive the great consolation that their Lord had promised them. For it was only after they had given up clinging to their Lord that his Spirit could descend into their hearts.

If mother's agony and death were indeed an agony and death with Christ, should I not then hope that she would also participate in the sending of the Spirit? The deeper I entered into my own grief, the more I became aware that something new was about to be born, something that I had not known before. I began to wonder if Jesus does not send his Spirit every time someone with whom we are connected by bonds of love leaves us.

To forget mother would be like forbidding her to send the Spirit to me, refusing to let her lift me up to a new level of insight and understanding of my life. I started to feel the power of Jesus' words: "It is for your own good that I am going because unless I go, the Advocate (the Spirit) will not come to you; but if I do go, I will send him to you. . . . When the Spirit of truth comes he will lead you to the complete truth" (John 16:7,13).

Is it for my own good that Jesus died, that my friends and relatives died, that my mother died? Am I able to affirm with my entire being that in and through Christ death has become the way by which the Spirit of truth comes to us? Must I grieve and mourn so that I will be ready to receive the Spirit when he comes?

These questions became very real to me in those confusing weeks after mother's death. I said to myself, "This is a time of waiting for the Spirit of truth to come, and woe unto me if, by forgetting her, I prevent her from doing God's work in me." I sensed that something much more than a filial act of remembering was at stake, much more than an honoring of my dead mother, much more than a holding on to her beautiful example. Very specifically, what was at stake was the life of the Spirit in me. To remember her does not mean telling her story over and over again to my friends, nor does it mean pictures on the wall or a stone on her grave; it does not even mean constantly thinking about her. No. It means making her a participant in God's ongoing work of redemption by allowing her to dispel in me a little more of my darkness and lead me a little closer to the light. In these weeks of mourning she died in me more and more every day, making it impossible for me to cling to her as my mother. Yet by letting her go I did not lose her. Rather, I found that she is closer to me than ever. In and through the Spirit of Christ, she indeed is becoming a part of my very being.

I am back at work now: teaching, reading, writing, laughing and getting angry. It all seems the same as five weeks ago. But things are not the same. Mother has died and it was for my own good that she left. I speak less and less about her, even my thoughts are less involved with her—yet I have not forgotten her. Remembering her now means a greater willingness to receive the Spirit of truth and to see more clearly my own vocation.

There is so much darkness to be dispelled, so much deceit to be unmasked, and so many ambiguities to be resolved. Mother's death is God's way of converting me, of letting his Spirit set me free. It is all still very new. A great deal has happened in these weeks, but what will happen in the months and years ahead will be far more than I can now understand. I am still waiting, yet already receiving; still hoping, yet already possessing; still wondering, yet already knowing.

Sometimes I find myself daydreaming about radical changes, new beginnings and great conversions. Yet I know that I must be patient and allow her who taught me so much by her life to teach me even more by her death.